NOTHING YOU CAN CARRY

NOTHING YOU CAN CARRY

SUSAN ALEXANDER

thistledown press

©Susan Alexander, 2020
All rights reserved

No part of this publication may be reproduced or transmitted in any form or by any means, graphic, electronic or mechanical, including photocopying, recording, or any information storage and retrieval system, without permission in writing from the publisher or a licence from The Canadian Copyright Licensing Agency (Access Copyright). For an Access Copyright licence, visit www.accesscopyright.ca or call toll free to 1-800-893-5777.

Thistledown Press Ltd.
410 2nd Ave. North
Saskatoon, Saskatchewan, S7K 2C3
www.thistledownpress.com

Library and Archives Canada Cataloguing in Publication
Title: Nothing you can carry / Susan Alexander.
Names: Alexander, Susan. 1957- author.
Description: Poems.
Identifiers: Canadiana 20200280813 | ISBN 9781771871983 (softcover)
Classification: LCC PS8601.L348 N68 2020 | DDC C811/.6—dc23

Cover photograph, *Cape Roger Curtis Stars,* by Emmett Sparling
Cover and book design by Jackie Forrie
Printed and bound in Canada

 Canada Council   Conseil des Arts
for the Arts   du Canada

Thistledown Press gratefully acknowledges the financial support of the Canada Council for the Arts, SK Arts, and the Government of Canada for its publishing program.

for Ross

Contents

Vigil

12	Anthropocene
13	Eschatology
14	Presence
15	Apologue
16	Visitation
17	Purgation
18	Apocrypha
19	Verily Verily
20	Clamavi
22	Threnody
23	Aletheia
24	Theophany
25	All Souls Day, Bowen Island
26	Canticle for Sea Lions in Howe Sound

Confession

28	Anchorite
29	Secret Cove, Sechelt Peninsula
30	Behind the Door
31	If Father was a Tree in the Boreal Forest
33	Ceremonies
35	Making Beds with Cordelia at the Avalon Motel in Osoyoos: Summer 1973
37	Annunciation
38	Matryoshka, Nesting Doll
39	Broody
40	Blessings for the Nights I Can't Sleep

41	Photograph Albums
42	Fog
43	Self Portrait
44	Late, Again

Parables

48	Colourblind Son
50	Gone is the Brave Little Tailor
51	Joringel
52	The Cinnamon Bird
53	Fisherman
54	Rose-Red
55	The Pooka
56	Youngest Son
57	On the Glass Hill
58	Young Huntsman
60	Convolvulus
61	The Monochrome World Loses the Light
62	Winter Rain
63	Echo
64	The Goose-Girl
66	Nightingale
67	At the Group Home

Pilgrimage

70	Maîtresse, Les Bories
71	Anatolia
72	There
73	Molino, San Antimo
74	Sevilla

75	Kasbah du Toubkal
76	Hemoglobin
77	Chuckanut Drive
78	Kissing
79	Introit
80	Advocate
81	Aubade
82	When you dream beside me
83	Prayer for Moon and Rain

Matins

86	Planet B
87	After Reading
88	Moving Home
90	The Otter
91	A Chandelier of Sex and Propagation
92	Commerce
93	Stop Me If You've Heard This One
94	The Developer's Curse
95	The Environmentalist's Curse
96	The Whirlwind Questions Burnco Rock Products Ltd. (regarding its environmentally-certified pit mine which will dredge 20 million tonnes of sand and gravel from the McNab Creek Estuary in Howe Sound, B.C.)
97	Sword Ferns in Spring
98	Theophany
99	Kashkul, Beggar's Bowl
100	Last Morning

choosing,
over heaven,
this common patch of earth

— Lorna Crozier, "Star Cluster"

Vigil

Anthropocene

I miss the old gods, before they slipped into the bunker.
Brace of doves, sifting through ashes. Before Google.
It's all DIY these days of data mining.
No kneeling fern deep beside the stream, no sprinkled water
before the drink. I don't remove my shoes.

The ocean too warm this summer.
I swam every day under wildfire smoke.
Thousands of jellyfish, full moons, drifted below.

Satellites caliper California's orange groves.
In a TEDX talk on YouTube, my friend the scientist
speaks about irreversible compaction of aquifers.
Unseen structures collapse,
pumped dry.

Beneath us the gods shift on molten thrones.
What to do about ghosts if the Styx runs low?

I am ever so mildly environmental.
Sign letters, petitions, mites sent to the cause.
Others fund apocalypse.
Temple stone cut and stacked in the warehouse. Listen.
The flawless red heifers in feedlots lament.
Outside the rail cars wait.

Check out old Kronos. He limps from the labyrinth
on the arms of his chums, Our Father
crisp in pleats, white leather gloves.
A sweet boy tumbles towards us on juicy pink legs.
Kiss him with alchemical lips,
swallow him whole.

Eschatology

for W.L.S. and the loved others

In the new forest, it is the young who die,
and the dying wear their hair long.
Braids trail down from dwindling limbs.
Moss wraps skirts around slim trunks.

The dead remain standing, held in the arms
of mothers, sisters, grandfathers.
Lungwort scales the tree bark,
holds a chartreuse light.

This life from loss. This living
plaited with the dead.
Lichens climb earth to sky,
clasp the boles with a thousand hands.

Touch me, says death.
I am soft and green as spring.

Presence

Outside the cabin,
the cedar shimmers.
No wind.
Air heavy with rain,
but no rain falls.
Just scintillation, vibration
scarcely visible.

Messages that don't depend
on tongue or touch.
Knowledge like scent
breathed in.
Water drawn to root.

This dark cope shelters
what may be
and what is possible beyond
what is.

Apologue

My great granddaughter put a wisp of blue
in my palm. She asked *what is this?*
She wouldn't tell me where she'd found it.
It took me awhile to remember
the word. Feather.

Once, I told her, when I was
a little girl, birds flew through the air
and built nests in trees. Each had its own
tune and plumage. Some were green,
some blue, some scarlet and others
were brindled, grey and brown.
Their colours were made of feathers.

What happened to the birds? she asked.

One day, all over the world, the birds
stopped singing. They began to fade.
You could see through their bodies.
Then they were shadows. Then, gone.
Next we felt a lightness come,
a hollow form inside our bones.

Visitation

I am lying on the deck trying to organize the stars
when I smell him. Something like engine oil,
then the rum and coke. Unmistakable. He says

Do you remember how to find the Little Dipper?

I don't. I'd forgotten the rough edge of his voice,
like he was trying to start something. He holds
his hands up huge against the sky and I can see the stars
through them. He moves the great wheel around the centre.

See, there, Polaris, he says, *it's the tip of the handle.*

All I can do is jab my fingers between cedar planks
to stop from lifting into night.

Purgation

The washing machine churns
into white. A noise like and not like
waves on the beach below.
The totems seem to turn,
to watch my house.
Its back door latched.
Conscience outside — a feral cat.
Halfhearted, I make to leave,
packing up etchings and photographs
into boxes heavy with blame.

                Heron, when you
come for me, your voice like stone
break. Take half the heart I have.
Take heart. Shape me a hut
where winter streams into the bay,
driftwood for shelves for shells for dishes.
Water from creek from rain from tears.
A bear   a doe   a breath   a bird.
Here in my hair   in my sainted hand.

Apocrypha

Rain is the language of God. How God engages the angels.
There was rain before we humans jumped up from the mud,
before a leaf appeared in the canopy,
before the house sparrow or Leviathan.

At one time, God and the angels gossiped perpetually.
So much so that the whole earth drowned.
That was long ago.
Nowadays they barely talk at all.

Verily Verily

Summer's mouth is over
burdened with sweet fruit.
Raspberries, everbearing
strawberries, blueberries,
cherries, red almost black.
Eating feels like a duty.

The blazing children
at beach picnics feed on
waves and shrieks
until smoke from wildfires
obscures the sun.

Faded oceanspray turns
the cliffside terracotta.
Scabbed vultures
graze the house windows
with wingtips.
Eight of them, circling.

Fallen and spent
is the foxglove's husk.
We are all of us leaving,
and the earth,
what will the ruined earth make
of this stale seed?

Clamavi

God, I am praying to you the morning after
        nineteen of the hottest years on record
        in the history of Your created earth where
        I am walking through the valley of the shadow.

God, I am praying to You to take Your people back
        because we like sheep have gone astray.

Take us back to 1839. Make us listen
        to Edmond Becquerel when he built
            the first solar fuel cell.

Take us back to 1888, those first wind turbines
        which for decades would power
            remote ranches and farms.

Take us back to 1892 when Boise, Idaho
        used hot springs to heat its homes,
        built the huge geothermal swimming pool
            on Warms Springs Avenue.

And since I am already on my knees praying, could You also,
        while You're tinkering with dates, delay
        a century or two that January explosion in 1901
        when Spindletop shot black gold into the blue Texas sky
            and the new century found its idol and its engine?

I know that time means nothing to You
        up there in eternity, but down here
        where our days are like the withering grass,
            we are running out of it.

I lift up to You not only our petroleum sins,
> but also by-product spinoffs and our plastic iniquities of
>> polyester, spandex, hearing aids, heart valves,
>> fishing rods, milk jugs, cortisone, crayons,
>> hot tubs, fertilizer, shampoo, paraffin,
>> bike tires, car tires, insecticide, aspirin,
>> ballpoint pens, cling wrap, wax paper, shaving cream,
>> eye glasses, contact lenses, tennis rackets, ink,
>> artificial turf, artificial limbs,
>> Vaseline and Maybelline, shoe polish, paint,
>> vitamin capsules, water pipes, toothpaste,
>> pillows, detergent, life jackets, lipstick,
>> combs, yoga mats, garden hoses and golf balls.

Save us O Lord
> from our sins of omission
>> and consumption
>> and commission.

Take us back O God and save Your sheep
> if this time we promise to give thanks
> for free wind and free water and free sunshine
> that blows and shines and rains on the rich and the poor,
>> the just and the unjust.

Lead us not into temptation,
> but make us to calm down,
>> to lie down, at last,
>>> in your green pastures.

Threnody

Lean into the oboe. Wail.
Water the roses, the scented ones.
Would you go backwards if you could?

Lock up the china, unsay the gibe,
leave suede shoes new in their box.

Miss the brother's tyranny,
held by a thread above the stairs.
Yet never fall down in the hayfield,
never fall up into blue.

To miss heartwrack, that mattock.
But also never to lick the milk drip
from lips unlatched, meet the gaze,
unwavering, of the glorious other.

You've been writing this poem for decades,
rewinding time until you don't exist.

You seek a peace like an underground sea.
Painless. Blind. A time before breath,

before soul's ravenous descent.

Aletheia

The beach path ends
in a charred ring,
the winding staircase
gone — its rot now
cinders among pebbles.
Low clouds shut down the day
before it begins.

No wind. Just the dark
breath of cedar and hemlock.
The waves flatten and dissipate
before they meet the shore.
The only sounds
    wing-flutter
    and a steady drip.

And because we turn away,
we are left to count out
days and ribs,
sift the ash for burned bones
and sighs. Because we turn away,
we skirt the garden god
hidden in salal. Search
in places we are certain
nothing will be found.

Theophany

If God were a tree, this page
could be a sacred thing,
oblation in cellulose.
Words would rustle,
stir heartwood,
cause water to rise
root to crown.

We'd toss seeds at weddings.
Every tap and stream
where we drink
would be holy.

If God were a tree,
we'd study Botany
to grow closer to
Divinity.
Our third eye
would be a leaf.

All Souls Day, Bowen Island

I am outside on the covered deck,
drinking coffee in the shadows with God.

Rain rackets off the tipped burn barrel.
Last night I stayed home from the party, watched

an improbable rom-com that hadn't aged well:
football shoulders and feathered hair.

Even so it was a relief to wander aimless awhile.
Grey light grows in the east, behind Gardner.

We listen for the humpback's slow breath. I rerun
my dread: low blood count, losing my beloved, woe.

You could go first, says God.
We both laugh, for a while.

Canticle for Sea Lions in Howe Sound

Did I tell you they wake me in the dark
with barking? They float the day away,
close-knit, a raft with flippers raised.
A sail past. Sea lions, prodigious and close,
show up after the herring spawn on Hornby.
I've never seen so many in the bay.

I want to tell you about my friend
who came over after work to forget
some bad news. *Why are they here?*
we wonder. Three dozen start porpoising.
Looking down from the cliff, we see
a sequinned splash, a breaking wave of anchovy.
Gulls blizzard above, a whirl and cry.

All the while permits are issued for industry:
gravel mine at the McNab estuary,
LNG at the Woodfibre site.
This, after expensive decades mopping up.
But I tell you, we must celebrate.
We must celebrate the return
in this place of herring and anchovy,
the salmon that follow, the dolphins, the whales.

For what I speak is both protest and praise,
witness to the living and the dying,
to the present return and the probable destruction.
So I must lie awake with my window open, listen
there   now   can you hear them?

Confession

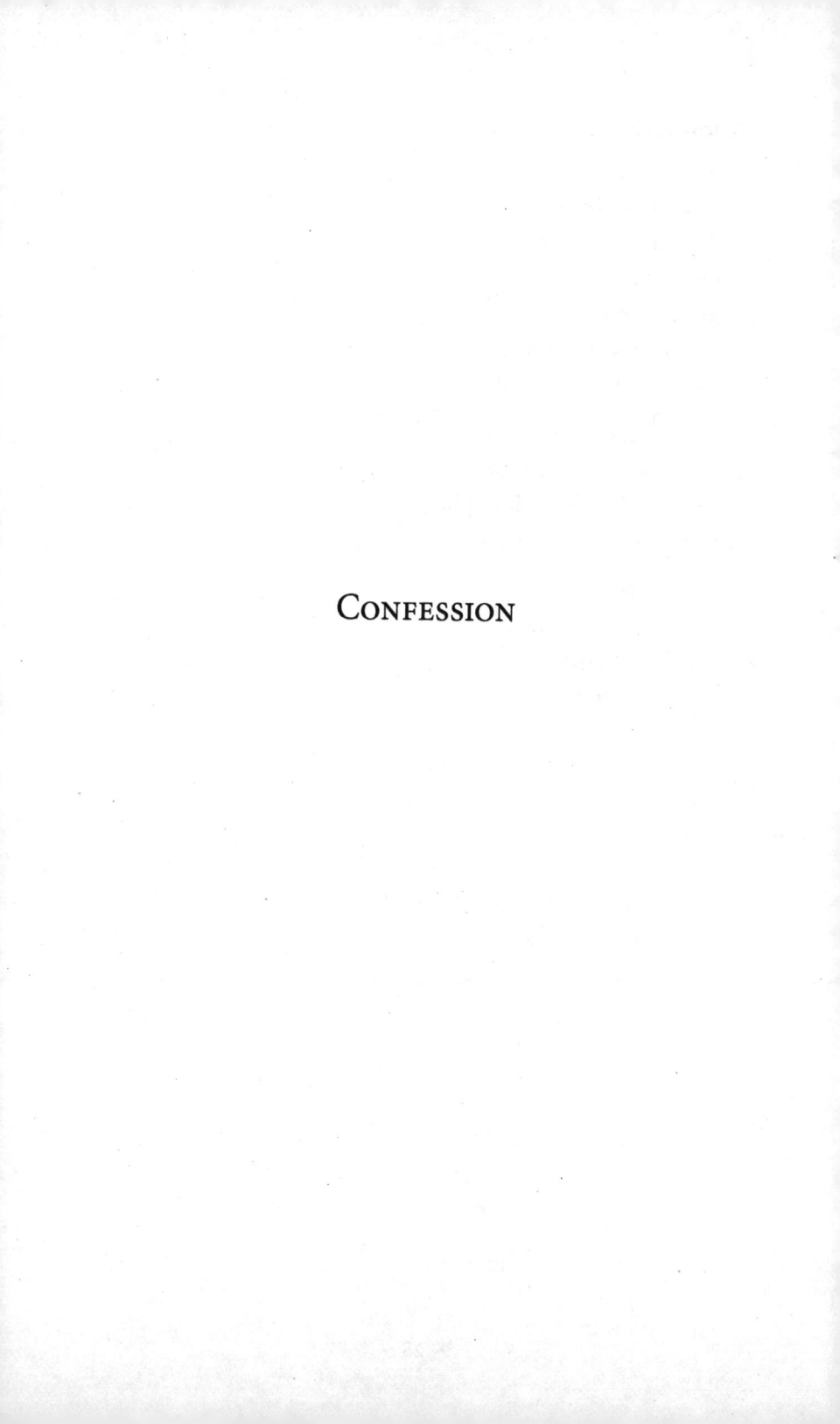

Anchorite

A door on the landing
at the top of the stairs.
Sometimes there.
Sometimes not.
Nothing so remarkable
as its own disappearance.

Behind it, only broken things.
A music box, electric train,
a ballerina, her dolly chin split
into matronly benevolence.

The possible door
blanked into wallpaper.
A staircase, a landing,
a row of empty shelves.

Secret Cove, Sechelt Peninsula

For millennia we drift with plankton—
with dinoflagellates and protozoa on ocean's gyre.
Boundless, our body, our mind bends
around horizons and hemispheres.
We are many.

At the moment of first singularity
it is moonless and July. A wooden boat at anchor.
A man and a woman slide off the stern
without a splash.

They glide through water stars, under
sky stars. How they shine!
We choose her for her radiance,
her ribboned limbs, rolling and stroking.

                The I who I am becoming
enters her with water, spermatozoa, with salt,
a last flash of light, because she,
she carries the sea inside herself. O Mother.

Behind the Door

The ache wakes her,
her breasts so hard and tender.
Something wrong with the nipples.
How they pull inside her
when she's cold
like fists.

If it isn't breasts, it's hips.
Femurs lengthen in the dark hours.
At times, she limps.
The socket
no longer fits.

Changeling.
Legs so long, she peers
into the eyes of the elders,
combs hair across her face.

Tears and blood,
she hadn't asked for this.
Childbody lost
as if fairies raided the night.
Left her with this stranger.

In the moonlight,
when bones grow,
when fur spreads
like moss over crevice,
when secrets bleed
into sheets, she presses
an edge, just there,
sharp, against
her own absence.

If Father was a Tree in the Boreal Forest

Let's say he was a sugar maple,
drawing up water for me to drink.
Roots in cracks in granite shield,
raising draughts sky high
from lake from creek from beaver pond.

Let's say he held my brothers and sisters,
the lot of us. We'd be his keys,
we'd hang off branches,
rock away summer's breeze until the leap.
Tiny helicopter children
in double samaras twirl
and a thousand scarlet hands clap our turning.

Say I could hear the mud song
below the register of birds —
violet and columbine,
the chorus of trillium, those holy innocents.
The cold-blooded tune
of the salamander and the little green snake.

Say I learned to stand still from him,
give only sugar when the spile
pierced the phloem.
Compare these lines on my palms,
my five fingers with this leaf.

My faith would be like his, like Solomon's,
in seasons, the greening time
and the time of fire walking.
The snow death which is not death
but a walking naked through black and white.

Let's say father was a sugar maple
and I awoke just one day
to a sweetness in my mouth.

Ceremonies

I was fifteen when
I planned my first funeral —
I mean my own.

Was more convinced by
death's certainty than
any future I could see

and it seemed far more
likely at the time.
Simpler. I designed

a dress of cotton gauze,
blonde hair combed smooth
to my waist, a daisy crown,

my feet were bare.
Open coffin, of course.
What they'd do is sigh

over this long lily of a girl
with lilies in her hands.
My name means lily

so perhaps I am
somehow more
readily made for death.

Finally they'd all feel
a proper regret
with Procol Harum singing

"A Whiter Shade of Pale."
They'd all be sorry,
wouldn't they? For what

they did and did not do.
Especially my parents.
Especially the beautiful

careless boy I loved
(at least a year) who
could not love me back.

Making Beds with Cordelia at the Avalon Motel in Osoyoos: Summer 1973

She could sing Desperado just like Linda Ronstadt.
I showed her hospital corners and how to
smooth sheets like my mother taught me.
She didn't have one — a mom.

Thrown out of the house — for nothing
according to her and I believed her,
believed the worst of fathers in general,
temper tantrums, hard hands and drinking.

She wouldn't talk about him, not a thing,
but I remember something about two bitchy sisters —
one with a name like venereal disease
while Cordelia,
        she walked right out of a magazine
with her long legs and sort of private smile —
smart too though she didn't show off like I did
or mouth off either.
                I taught her how to
tuck a bedspread under pillows then curve it
snug like a tight T-shirt. She had the knack.

When she wasn't around I tried
to talk and dress and wear my hair like her,
be patient with my little niece, be nicer
than I was or am.
              She lived alone
in our trailer out back of the motel
beside the slough we called a lake —
saving up for university she said.

Sometimes after work we'd lie together
under the walnut tree. I'd play with her hair
while she read *Tess* — rich green leaves
breaking the heat of an Okanagan afternoon.

I always thought she'd get discovered
like that dairy queen girl, that she'd marry
a millionaire.   Strange thing is

I was the one who kind of made it in the end,
the one with the house and European holidays.
But Cordelia,

       she was making her way for awhile,
then somehow it went bad again — a man,
some dark angel, following her.

Annunciation

She opens the blinds, stretches out alone
in a stranger's bed. Outside the window,
night clings. Pines dim the first grey light.
Something is there. A form, a face swivels
towards her. Perfectly awake
in diminishing shadow, she sees a truth,
its round head and barred silence.

         It is as if
someone enters her then, something moves
inside her, knows who she is. Not because
she is uncommon, but because she is lost
and watching. It preens its belly,
pinions spread and ready. She stares
at the emptiness where it perched
a moment, a minute, a wingspan ago.

Matryoshka, Nesting Doll

So big I can't sleep.
The baby's feet squeeze
air from my lungs. Three a.m.
I smell something
burning. Fire at the transfer
station across the street.
I call it in.

The smoke
wakes the old animal.
Bear. Bobcat. Wolf.
I hear the stars, their broken
music, the bulbs pushing
through frozen earth.
I hold all the ancestors
inside me.

Broody

The first time I held her unknown after
months hidden in my own darkness,
her skin was smeared with white pith,
nose pores etched and visible like papillae
on the tongue. Hers rooting,
blind. Strange pup. Mine, not
mine.

I'd always abhorred the flesh, craved
carved marble, the cool distance of
Descartes' pilot. Until this
human crooned an animal clamour
around the hospital cot.

She sung me a body she'd been
building within, called down a shriek
of milk through nipples grown long
and brown. Thick was my pelt below
the *linea nigra*, below the red web of
scars. My nails turned claw and
I could taste blood, knew I would kill
(rapaciously and with joy)
to shelter, to feed.

Her wrinkled fist opened in sleep,
cheek beaded with cream and I heard
the yip yip yip,
coyotes nipping along my veins.

Blessings for the Nights I Can't Sleep

I remember
when my daughters
tried to fool me
with pretend sleep.

I loved how
they'd fool themselves,
a stillness catching them up,
drifting each away until morning.

I lie in the night listening still
for their tiny sweet breaths,
moth wings
dusty with sleep.

Photograph Albums

if you believe them it was one perpetual holiday in the sun
from beginning to endless white beaches stretching
past Peponi's hotel on the Indian Ocean
to washed silver   Oregon's coast in September light

                      perfect children lifting kites

here we row row row our boat gently down the Thames
through Wind in the Willows to the Beetle and Wedge and yet
on the Ridgeway path someone's heart breaks

                      we smile for the camera

see these   plastic sheets adhere   peel and remove
a hand   a face   a family   in the end like us
    they expose

                    disintegration

Fog

An immaculate wall closes off the bay
where she sits in a thin quilt. Clouds
and an empty cup. Crying gulls
and the smell of wet cedar.
The drone of a plane is swallowed by whiteness
which is how her world erases itself.
She tries to understand the waves, the way
they paraphrase water. Maybe, she thinks,
she has become like him. Reading the end
of the novel first. Whatever she reads next
has already happened.

Self Portrait

Saxophone blows in blue skies,
blows in rain. I'm writing again
by the light of the fridge.
My father's fist, at the end of my arm,
makes the cutlery jump.
Oceans between my ears.
These feet outgrew
all my sisters' pretty shoes.

Late, Again

I don't see it numbered among the seven deadlies. My mother named me late bloomer, which means I've been slow to my own arrival. I spend every day playing tag with myself.

Being late is rarely personal. I'm a startled flock of birds, a black cloud turning. Time itself is at fault. It stretches out in all directions, loops into yesterday and vaults into tomorrow. Then it's gone like an empty roll of toilet paper.

Let me number the echelons of lateness: first date, final exam, specialist appointment, sister's wedding, papal audience. Some cluster around a single event: missing the last ferry to the island or the plane with connections — Munich to Marrakesh.

Some people link tardiness with *The Creative Mind*, an otherworldly listening into murmurs from the ether, but that comes close to boasting.

Is there a saint I can pray to? Will Boniface do, patron of Germany? No.
Pray then to Saint Expeditus. Centurion, excoriator of procrastination, come to me with your sword.
Kill the raven who whispers to me: *later.*

I missed my mother's last breath.

                                            The dog needed walking and the couch needed lying upon. I needed a fight, some cathartic shouting and the making up afterwards. Understand me gentle reader. The bronze fountain understands and weeps its ceaseless tears. As do the angels, detectable by the scent of lilacs, a cherished flower of she who has left us.

Could I blame my sister, #5 in the family, who left before I swanned in? How I want to say that it was I, #7, last and favoured child, who caught her final breath like the good daughter who crowds the hospice room for days with a competitive patience.
Did her brown eyes (see I have them too, her father's above-the-arctic-circle eyes — her mother's were blue as Norwegian beach glass), did they open at the last to a blank chamber?

She lies freshly dead, still warm under the handmade quilt (sister #3). I touch the arm that cancer turned to eggplant. Aubergine, a more elegant word. I won't eat that vegetable again.

Time rings a still pool around her deadness. There is no one to be late for now. Nothing to fit in optimistically between excess tasks. #5 appears and #4 (my brother, bereft of gibe and banter). We border her with heat and *yea though I walk through the valley of* breath whose body cools beneath the incandescent lamp.

The doctor finds me wandering the hallway. She waves a free pass like a benediction. *Sometimes our watching tethers the dying*, she says. *They often make an exit while we fix a cup of tea.*

Nurses refuse time's slow number.
They hover above this silence on white linen wings.

Parables

Colourblind Son

Years ago she showed him a copy of Brueghel's
The Blind leading the Blind and explained
how the artist chose faded pigments
to play up his subject. She insisted
they were almost
seeing the same painting.

Just as she told him that they see
the same world in twilight
and in winter
when cold hammers down the colour range
to soot and light, to tones of tan and khaki.

It is not important to the young man
that his mother should understand
the palette he inhabits.
He does not tell her
that the riotous hues she sees
are all in her head anyway,
figments of her own overblown perception.

When he brings a girl home for Sunday lunch,
his mother praises
her Titian hair and green eyes, but to him
she is all the soft shading of a wood dove.
She holds a pose and he draws her with charcoal.

Afterwards they walk in November rain
and watch the dark salmon
belly their slow way upstream.
He points out
the texture of river stones, the layers
of fallen leaves and the two deer motionless
who look back at them from the bush.

Gone is the Brave Little Tailor

You are not he
whose needle shaped
so many appearances.

You are the one
who would not
pit wits against giants,
who dared not win the princess.
The one who would not
rise from a dinner table
littered with bones and flies
to walk north through twilight
and starlight toward the peaks.

You are the one who remains
behind blinds
in the basement room,
and yet sews clothes for others.

Outside the window,
air shudders before rain begins.
If, if, if, insists a hidden bird. If.

In a scarlet purse,
stitched with silver thread,
you carry your song.
It sags with all
that might have been.

Joringel

And so he lost her as shadows fell across
the meadow beside the barbed wire fence.

For years he drifts between towns
working for bed, food, a fix. Every night
the same dream. Her hand reaches for his
in twilight and he is turned to stone.
He wakes to his strange body, rigid.
Always he studies faces — the waitress
at the diner, so tired, the woman
standing scarecrow in her garden.
When he walks, he picks up whispers,
glimpses — birdsong, flower, pearl.

In the woods, tree fungus flares
like lace. Such delicate ears listening
for summer's slow approach. What he wants
is to go back to before her eyes went dark.

In his dream, he finds Lady's Mantle,
a leaf that cups a bead of dew.
He brings it to the school's iron gate. A touch
and each lock springs open. Doors swing
into a dormitory of birds, silent in cages.
His arms stretch open until the sky is filled
with wings, the morning throbs with song.
She stands taller than him now. Eyes alight.

The Cinnamon Bird

One fall, when the leaves turned colour,
a bird came and trilled a cadenza
for three I loved,
As it sang, their bodies curled into themselves.

Two years later, the bird came back,
this time for my daughter's lover.
It was spring. The lilacs bloomed.

Yesterday it returned
to perch on the cedar branch
outside my sister's summer house.
Her rooms lilt with its singing.

When the bird comes, the world light turns red.
The heart stops beating.
When it leaves, it takes the seasons with it.

Fisherman

his wife is a purse of want
a swallower of kingdoms
she tosses at night
her body swells into tempest
tears up the shore

the fisherman knows
nothing can be enough
he slits the belly
throws the guts into black waves

she eats the fish he serves
a meal of fried white flesh
he lifts fork to lips
wipes flakes from her chin
his fingers twist her loose rings
round and round
until she sleeps at last

he sits on stone
outside the door
mends his nets
he lists toward the sea

Rose-Red

I am a king's son, he said, and I was bewitched.

I kept the pelt. It was the colour of my hair,
smelled ripe as a rowan tree.
Alone in my stateroom, I wrestled
his bearskin from the chest,
buried my face in fur and remembered
my mother's cottage, winter nights
beside the hearth, toying
with that dark storm.

The wooden door shattered on broken
iron hinges. I loped through
the open gate, beyond the screams, swifter
than any pony, through bush and bramble as if
called to this clearing. Morning mist rose
and I too stretched up
higher, higher. My nails
tore through bark like knives
through butter, and I roared.

After that came snow and the quiet.
Hare, roe, stag, badger in its sett.
I could hear bees hum
deep inside their cluster, smell
a trace of summer's
honey. I'd never felt so warm.

At last, came the long sleep.
In branching dreams, I search
for bilberries, their shine of wild jewels,
behind a hedge my mother
prunes her roses.

The Pooka

November is a white horse
horned with the young moon.
Over a bridge the fool capers
starlit and music drunk.
He tumbles along and off
the path, through
a gate into circled stone.

Pole star whirls
a dance of brambles
and shadow
over frosted grass
where on his back the fool sings.

Round and round him
bare feet leap in time
with the tune. Charmed
hands toss bright coins.

The winter wren
and tattling wind
rouse first light
where the fool lies
asleep beneath
his gold, a hoard
of pale leaves, scattering.

Youngest Son

He remembers the brush whipping
his face and the red flame tail
that carried him over stock and stone
faster than the horse he stole,
faster than wind, than thought.

Only now, with everything brimming
around him golden, does the boy
understand. Quick as desire,
the fox is there.

Shoot your arrow
through my heart.
Cut off
my head and my feet.

Trembling, the boy does, and so
the fox changes to the man. Perfectly
still. A held feather quivers

over red lips and he kisses him-
self awake as naked as sunrise
as summer as a wedding day song
that sings of a happiness as life is long.

On the Glass Hill

What father lifts
his transcendental daughter
to make of her an altarpiece.
What daughter does not want
her father's heart
even when it's made of glass.
Half the kingdom is an unlikely prize
unless indeed she is half of what he has.

Above her the black swans
circle the woods, cross the fjord.
She plots to run off
with the charcoal maker,
a lad of soot and tatters who burns
with a patient heat.
To him she tosses all she holds
in her lap, her golden apples.

Her father sits in his tower
counting diminishing returns.
He takes her face from its frame,
feeds it to the shredder.
Against blind windows,
the grass grows high and wild.

Young Huntsman

Before the sunrise shows
rabbit tracks in silver
grass, he waits,
hidden in his blind.
A thin shine along
the pond's face,
along the arrow's shaft.
Out of nowhere, a crackle,
the old mother. He shares
bread with her, knowing
how the story goes.
A wishing cloak, the heart
of a dead bird swallowed
whole. Under his pillow
every morning after,
a piece of gold.
And the pleasure years
pass so quickly —
he throws it all away.
Mistakes for love a sleight
of hand, a trick of light.
He tightens the noose,
exact and extract.
Floats, high
on that storm.

Come cloudburst,
he spills again to earth.
Every bone snaps. And the crone
comes as she always will.
Breaks open a cabbage
from her garden, feeds him
bitter leaves. At the gate,
the dead bird sings.

Convolvulus

When they meet,
      he wears a coat
           of morning glories.
      Each flower drags
the sky closer.
      She is unraveled
           by blue eyes.
      Never has she known
such a blooming.
      He climbs into her
           arms, vines twine
      through curls. Kiss
and tendrils enter
      lips, slip down
           her windpipe, twist
      round her liver,
twirl over bones.

The Monochrome World Loses the Light

Winter city has set its trap.
Snow hedges her inside.
Frost scratches messages
onto windowpanes,
the black-boned trees snap.
She forgets how to dress.
She wants to lie down in the curve
of the river. There
where sky is boundless,
where come spring
snowdrops will breathe
between her ribs.

Winter Rain

A body appears in the bathroom mirror.
She is startled to see the slender
shape nothing makes.
She dresses carefully over that hollow space
and catches a bus into the city,
hat and jacket cupped around her
phone, the outerworld, lit up.

Covertly, she composes
petal words and earth tunes
to quiet the buried ones who push up
through the long dark.

What she hears behind the music:
raindrops falling on rhododendron leaves,
her footsteps on the road
between sleeping houses.

Echo

She, who has been hunted
by the goat-footed lover, is haunted by
that rough wooing. She hides in the valley
with her sisters and her fierce mother.
Safe — as a woman is safe.

He wanders in, accidentally.
Incurious of flesh, except his own.
He lacks interest in her science:

> the way ferns unfurl as seahorses
> to ride the wet spring air,
> raven's thirty-three calls
> or how tentacles of light filter
> through the forest's colonnades.

It is no surprise she is attracted.
She wants him because
he does not want her,
particularly. For him,
any domestic will do.

His house is breathless with possessions:
gilded lamps teeter on stacked first editions.

Slowly she polishes
herself into carved armoires,
between marquetry strips,
becomes the miniature
salt cellar coffered under glass.

Evenings she presses red-tipped
fingers against the window pane.
Its surface ripples.

The Goose-Girl

Belly pressed in sedge
hands sunk in mud
face wet in the stream
at last she can drink
more than any cup
can hold.

Her mother's blood
cries warning but she lets
the handkerchief slip
into the flow. The pulse
she hears in her jaw
is her own.

It is because she falls
in love with an open world
beyond stone walls,
beyond silk and oracle.
Let the friend betray her.

Let the goose-girl sing
up a breeze to catch
the farm boy's hat
and make him race.

It is because she falls
in love with the wind
when it teases her hair
as she combs and braids.
How it shakes the tree
from the root.

She wants to know
where it comes from
and where it goes.
She wants to move
like that. Unseen.

Nightingale

The bejewelled
fake is silent, broken
beside the bed
where the great man dies.
He doesn't call for her,

but from the magnolia in bloom
at his window, she sings away death
from his chest. He doesn't deserve it.

Once upon a time, it seems to me,
every Christina, Hans and Oscar
heard Philomela ecstatic
in the woods
and was saved.

I listen to birdsong
caged inside this glittering laptop.

Child,
you there outside,
can you hear her singing?

At the Group Home
for Chris

Everyday we make these coffee cup sleeves out of leather
and it gets real quiet.
It's like there's snow falling on me   but it isn't cold.
It's falling inside me too.

I used to know how to fly.
I'd get running fast you know   and suddenly   flying.
No mind   just feathers and wind.

I like feeding the crows here.
Those two on the shed.
That one's Carlos and the other's his Yaqui teacher.

Back then we were questing for the grail.
Where are the other knights? Other knights. The knights.
Knights. Knights.
They're gone dark except sometimes
I hear shouts   and I can't run anymore.
It's okay, it's okay, it's okay.   It's okay.

My brother lives down the street.
How come he's older than me now? Bald old man. It's okay.

I gave a girl my soul   to keep it   safe.
I put it in a bear   the size of my hand
that I made   that I made   out of sheepskin.
I can't remember her name. What does she look like?
Look. Look.
It's okay. It's okay.

I like feeding the crows. Those two   there.

Pilgrimage

Maîtresse, Les Bories

Scatter-children flung like seeds
we come from forever to this house.
Windows an arm's reach through masonry.
Swifts fly through brick to their chimney sleep.

Duller birds tussle, like us, under wisteria leaves.
A few second blooms among all the jade pods,
exclamation marks hung in the arbour.

We return because she knows
how to feather stone beds, how to feed
the needs of these who nest here.
Sauter. Émincer. Fouetter. Goûter.
Words build wax spires and caverns
on the tablecloth among bottles and crumbs.

At daybreak the swifts screech,
strafing barn and window, wings tip to tip
while sleepers cry in waking dreams,
mouths open to the sabayon sky.

Anatolia

The tile makers of Iznik lost a dazzling red
four hundred years ago.
Someone died, the secret in his throat.
The absence of green in the leaf is death.
Spirit is structure left behind,
a fire hidden within the daily business.
How it hurts to see symmetry,
to know you are not meant for perfection.
The girl asks: *Are you good, or are you trying to be good?*
The boy answers: *Come.*
What you look for here is nothing you can carry home.
Home, where there are no shadows under blazing maples.
Only scarlet.

There

The child climbs the trees
that grow there —
wild orchards of them
beyond the old broken walls.
Fruit for every living creature.
Everbearing.

Knowledge is juicy,
soft as peach. Life, more
citrus. Different tastes
according to the season.

The child sits
among columbines —
those petalled rockets of fire.
She listens to earth's bone
Precambrian stone
and begins to hear
what it's been shouting
all these years.

Molino, San Antimo

To my eyes not different from the ones at home,
floating motionless in the villa pool.
Close by, chants loosed above abbey stone,
long sonorous prayers for the wants of the world.

You watched me lift it from the water.
So perfect. Such slender fingers.
How can something half aquatic drown? You swore
it was dead. Everywhere the scent of ripened vines.

I curled the body over a garden lamp, warm
in sunlight. Watched its infinite stillness. Waited
for a pulse at its throat.

I was in love with Cecilia then. She'd shipped
a barn to Alberta from Calabria, made it her home.
It was her sorrow that hungered me. Paneforte pilfered
from the kitchen. Olives from the swirled glass jar.

I didn't recognize my hand. And even amid
the wheels, the stream's dry bed, the millstone
with nothing left to grind, this small resurrection.

A salamander, gone.

Sevilla

What he wants is for me to go
see the sights in this scorched city
in a world he has already started,
I think, to leave.

On the roof of the cathedral,
tourists huddle under vaulting arches almost as high
as La Giralda, and I am buttressed by saints.

Plaza de España, haunted by children and ghosts.
See there, at the fountain centre,
moving within the spray, the conversos, the conquered,
lost spirits tethered.

The apartment door opens into quiet.
I cannot find him at first,
his face etched by jacaranda shadows.
It's like coming home from school
to someone eager to hear everything
I've learned today.

Inside the baker's box,
my crumbled magdalenas.

Kasbah du Toubkal

I used to think I could speak the language of animals.
Tonight in the high Atlas, while I dung out my sins
or lie slack in a foreign body, a dog will not stop barking.
She has a message to deliver, and she does it
wholeheartedly, without pause.
The rhythm rebounds down the valley,
off mountain shoulders, the cliff clinging walls of the Kasbah.

I am a sphinctered tube from mouth to anus, a worm
with arms and legs and head. A walking, talking decomposer.
My tongue is not one muscle but many, intertwined,
a flexible matrix like octopus arms,
with the same shape-changing acumen.

Intelligence, someone told me, is not wholly contained
in the cranium but scribed into the body's cells
from the libraries of nuclei and thereby
knitted into organ tissues and all along intestinal walls.
(Tonight the protracted abacus of my gut counts regrets.)

A cider scent rises from a hidden orchard.
The worm turns. Fossils of ammonites and ancient squid
shine darkly from the bathroom's marble slabs.
An ocean among desert peaks. Pictograph writings.
Another message of joy or extinction I cannot fathom.

The full moon illuminates boulders, precarious on the ridge,
crumbling peaks behind. The dog has stopped her barking.
When did that racket cease?
A wonder how peace and sometimes sleep
slip in unawares between thought and breath.

Hemoglobin

After countless tackles and concussions,
fist fights and spectacular crashes,
the heart continues its protracted drum solo,
      sonic bass line,
         electronic zombie trance dance vibe.
Did you ever think you'd live so long?

Highways, boulevards and capillaries.
FedEx trucks, pickups and deliveries.
      The Transportation Network on the Move!
Red lights circle the hubs,
streaming down corridors and arteries.

The product deteriorates.
What is your age in heartbeats?
      Yellow taxis begin to circulate.

Have you noticed the neighbourhood going downhill?
The slow bone marrow factories,
reduced hours and employees, disappearing
      benefits. Abandoned alleys.
So many driverless cars on the roads these days,
      yellow taxis with no clientele.

Chuckanut Drive

cliff curves on a Kawasaki   she   riding pillion
high up behind   hands strap the rider   enfolding   enthroned
lean left lean right   shadow and flash
bare legs race over blacktop   oyster bar passed
straddle and brace   trees stripe blind into blaze
banking turns and curve   green tunnel of shadow
lean right lean left

red-limbed the Bacchae sing between trees
drink surf   roar   the engine ecstatic
barefoot on needlestrewn dirt   hands twine in hair
wine teeth and wine palms   the flash and the blind
all singers attend the descent to the sea
she and the green pull the rider beneath   spill him wine dark
on wine-papered ground   his cheeks and chin
smooth as a woman   smooth as madrona skin
tongue over tunnel and curve   stripped and slipping
lean forward lean back

the chorus   the forest   the thyrsus   the thirst

thus halts the dance   it is fixed
the green portal closes   it is fate   the immortals turn
towards a lowering sky   the song glows and sinks red streamers
thrown against blue   and so accede   the antique climb
the drive unwind   the highway
through haze   into city night waste
straight   unto the end of days

Kissing

Teach me because
I never knew
how to except
chastely, dry brush on the brow
or a touch against stubble.

Even though my lips
are splendid and full,
smooth newborn skin,
I never learned to kiss.

I imagine it —
a slow dawn
spangles the clouds rose-pink,
silver polishes the bay.
But I fear
the spreading apart,

swallowing you down, so new,
so tender. You
sucked inside Charybdis,
ground meat caught
between metal crowns.

Sweet, teach me.
Teach me how
because
I never knew.

Introt

Because there is little frivolity
or vanity left on a shining dome —
akin to an ostrich egg,
that holy object hung
among the votives of the orthodox
church, or perhaps,
the full moon — his thoughts
must be more august,
his words more prophetic.

He is no statue, though the white
looks cool as marble. I write
upon that curved surface
with fingertips, fond lips.

This teaches me
to shed all the pretty things
that keep me from
the invisible world I am
moving towards.

Advocate

The whispers may prove true,
but tonight his large hands untangle me.

And I should give up this song
for a sorrow that is to come?
As all sorrows are to come if
they are not now.

He sleeps on my vast bed —
wings stretch wide into the night,
skin pierced by starlight.

Aubade

After we open each other   head to toe
I cannot so easily   close. I defy   my loss
even while you lie beside me. Always
I want   more   of the everything   I just owned.

I am an Imperialist   in love. I want
to occupy you   with my armies
claim every   wood and creek
of you. I want full   possession.

Yet   because I love
I allow you (lost in sleep now)   your darling
freedom   you'll never know
how close   you came
to losing.

When You Dream Beside Me

in the night
I will try
not to move.
I know sleep when it comes
comes lightly,
sleep of the cat,
whose feral ears twitch
whiskers alert for a change
in the weather.

You were so small when
you crept to your mother's bed.
Still as death
or sent away.
No touch. The white sheet
between you
an acre of snow.

Tonight I watch beside you
so silent
your hand in mine
forgets,
begins its sleep dance.
Better than dream
for me to know
the rose of your body
open,
your summer breath upon me.

Prayer for Moon and Rain

He is a shadow who sits at times at table with me. Today, clouds swallow him. Rain washes him naked and out to sea. Cold as a fish he slides between waves. This ghost of him remains.

O I would dress him in cashmere and sheepskin, buff his palms warm again. To see his smile is like catching a sliver of moon between clouds on a windy night.

No, he says. *What do you really mean?* I scrabble for words to cover me. How our small words hit like fists. How the one who holds the moon sees the midnight in me. My own tide rises and flows away. He asks *what's this atmosphere?*

His moonrise smile I snatch for myself, tuck it between leaves of a book. Rainstorm and sword fern turn the little light green. The maple's bones hold wet stars, falling offerings to the day.

As for love, the stream floods its banks and pours white down the beach cliff into the bay. Everything dancing.

His hands so cold under down, under cover. What will keep his heart from cooling now? His head a rainstorm, his face smooth carved stone.
O but my hands are brambles. They scratch and sting.

Darshana.
I come with nothing to offer
and wait for his risen eyes to see me. Make me whole.

MATINS

Planet B

All night the desert presses in.
Dry mountains and boulders, their heave and hang.
Everything watches us and we watch, helpless.

This fear is not the fear of death.
It's the zombie dread of being half alive and moving,
but tapped by another intelligence
for an unknown purpose.

Rain wakes me. I remember the world
where I live is still grasping to life.
Ferns breathe in sea brume.
Cedar rusts the ground.
The sun, a black pearl, won't be unveiled for days.
On the wall, a mask slowly opens its eyes and smiles.

After Reading

Something pushes
tumours through the black soil
of raised beds. Scarlet
eruptions from the underworld
split into wrinkled fists.

Is it only the rhubarb
thrusting out of the dark,
suddenly unfamiliar?

Its fetal strangeness,
its urgent need to be seen.

This is why you are afraid
in the night when
dreams unwind. Rise.

Moving Home

Last year I fell off
               the unrailed deck
       of the new house.

I was falling
       and falling
              like Alice.
       So slowly
              I even had time

to finish
       the poem
       I was reading
and drain
       my mug of coffee
              on the way
             down.

The packed boxes
                      were falling
       around me,
              their contents spilling
down the cliffside
       into
              a rising tide.

I didn't care
                anymore
about framed family photos
       or the dishes
       that smashed
              over barnacled rocks,

underwater
:::::::::::in eel grass
at home
:::::with the shiners
:::::I used to catch
when I was a girl.

The Otter

after Philip Levine

I think I must have lived
once before this life
as a pliable, sinuous otter
winding among all the shining yachts
at anchor or tied to the wharf
where ladies and gentlemen
in navy stripes and white-soled topsiders
bounce laughs across the bay
while I slide in and out of the stern unseen,
or seen only by children, soon forgotten.
It would explain my appetite
for Dungeness crab and the vibrissae
on my lip, chin and cheek
and how I see more clearly underwater.
It would explain how every surface
becomes dinner plate or berth
or place to defecate the remains —
crushed shells along mooring lines,
my slack wire specialty.
It would explain
my tendency to play with things
that do not belong to me
but to ladies and gentlemen
on wide decks and docks
who clink drinks beside seafood barbecues
who smile at my loops and twists
until I come too close with my grin
and my whiff of skunk and fish
so close they see my cuspids
and my lithe indifference.

A Chandelier of Sex and Propagation

Today (after I've washed the mason jars
and left the bay leaf, the bones,
the carrots, onions and celery tops
to simmer into soup stock on the stove)
I will plant a garden mix of lettuce seed.

With an empty cup I wander the long driveway
where catkins dangle from alders overhead —
light, winsome, wind-swung harbingers,
teaching me to be undead again
when the night loses its hold on hope
for dreaming.

I am looking for earthworms
to go in the raised beds, though the rain stopped
before dawn and the world's turned golden
with dust. Siskins send up flares of pollen.
What seemed to stretch and creep
are tree flowers fallen on blacktop.

It's been a long time now since I didn't know
I was killing the earth. Not just the diesel
parked over asphalt but the wanting more
while sighing over TV liars.

            I am gone far
underground to hide from those hungry birds,
my scruples. I pull out the weeds, bury my hands
in black dirt. Intend to be pure.

Commerce

The tidy stockbroker docks at the summerhouse wharf.
He lifts his daughter over the gunwales. They look down.
Under the surface, blue velvet mussels, the colonies
of acorn barnacles, anemones, Witches Hair waving
in the current, Turkish Towel and Sea Staghorn.

Every day plankton arrive and set up shop,
plant themselves along the steel cables and tire fenders.
Cirri filter sea water for drifters,
siphons inhale and exhale. A school of herring
jostles for a piece of that, a better position.

The man bends his crisp khaki knees,
picks up the pole scrubber.
An economy is lost.

Stop Me If You've Heard This One

An environmentalist and a land developer
go for a walk.

On the first trail,
they follow the creek to a stone hollow
furred with crane's bill moss and maidenhair.
Together they stoop at the pool and drink.
Is this the place? asks the environmentalist.
Nope, says the developer.

On the second trail,
they see the eagle's nest
and watch a pileated woodpecker
fly into the high cavity of a dead maple.
Is this the place? asks the developer.
Nope, says the environmentalist.

On the third trail, the two climb high
to an outcrop, beneath them,
a greenstone bluff. They look out
to the blue strait, blue sky,
towards the blue San Juans to the south.

Here lives the island's green heart,
says one, and the other smiles as if
to agree.

The Developer's Curse

May municipal workers spray weed killer through your garden's
    margin onto your carefully unmodified kale.
May you be sterile as the rapeseed Monsanto sells.
May you discover your home once housed a meth lab, that its
    gyprock walls exude fumes through the fresh coat of non-toxic
    paint.
May you sing your protest songs to town councils on retainer.
May you neglect your day job and lose it.
May your opinion become commodity, your ragtag lobby
    hawked to the highest bidder.
May you use your own people like plastic cutlery, your old
    ideals like Styrofoam plates serving up propaganda
    and overflowing the landfill.
May your hopes be felled like the old growth forests, your
    dreams fed to the chipper and turned to mulch for
    the footpaths that skirt my unsullied subdivisions.
May you live in one and end up loving it.

The Environmentalist's Curse

May your high-gloss phrases turn to spittle,
dribble down your chin. May your ever clever answers
twist to drivel, your lies plaque your arteries.

May your spin wizard, unpaid, at last pen the truth.
May your banker write you off as you wilt in your cot.
May the ones who sit with you be those you betrayed.

May they smile, hold your limp hand,
drone endlessly of mussel beds and green ways,
eel grass and red-listed species.

May alders sprout like arugula through the roads you
tarmacked. May stairstep moss fill cracks in the crazed
rock, maidenhair ferns find homes in your bore holes.

May your body be composted, dug deep
in the conservancy garden. May heirloom tomatoes
ripen as red as your choleric cheeks.

May they burst in the mouth with a succulent tang.

The Whirlwind Questions Burnco Rock Products Ltd. (regarding its environmentally-certified pit mine which will dredge 20 million tonnes of sand and gravel from the McNab Creek Estuary in Howe Sound, B.C.)

Behold now behemoth, which I made with thee. Job 40:15

Where were you when the peaks climbed
high above the sound? Can you speak
with a voice that quells the Squamish blow?
Is it you who tilts the waterskins, who swells
the stream into cascades, who calls home
the coho, dog, and pink? Can you vault
like the rainbow? Or scent creek pebbles,
rushed by earth's magnetic pull? Have you
offered meat for cougar, bobcat, bear?
For the eagle and the goshawk?
Can you hold this one small bud, forge
the arbor-vitae? Will you live the cedar's
thousand years? Have you shaped an egg
into red-legged frog or rough-skinned newt?
Does your body snare carbon
in sea sedge meadows? Have you heard
the elk calve under the canopy, her twins
hidden beneath the thimbleberry bush?
Have you the heron's skill, her stillness?
Can you, like the salamander,
restore a missing limb?

Sword Ferns in Spring

If you stop
(waist high hemmed in on every side)
and the wind stops
and the winter wrens quit
their frantic love trills, you may hear
a sound galactic —
how fractals unfurl in Fibonacci spirals,
how each frond learns those intervals,
sings variations on the theme.

Treble and bass clefs tip
fresh growth, trembling
along the staffs of winter veterans.
Golden cochleae listen for harmonies.
Tomorrow they will play the tune.

All winter they have endured for this.
The dead and the seasoned circle
new geometry.
Every year you must come
join the chorale, faithful and primordial.
Even you,
with your fretful grace note.

Theophany

What will you cook
for dinner if God arrives
one evening self-invited
with the usual entourage
of do-gooders who tut-tut
while they slip
down the hall to scrutinize
your Japanese erotica
enroute to the powder room?

What if the only thing
God hungers for is you?
Everything has a price
as you well know.
Whispers rise, hive
hum, bees circling.
Hush. Hush. Sweet smoke.

Every palm fills with gold
except yours.
Hosanna.
High above your head
hands wave
empty — alive — open.

Kashkul, Beggar's Bowl

First quarter moon in the sky with just a few wispy clouds in deepening blue. How is it all the cars on the Lions Gate Bridge don't stop? How come drivers and passengers don't walk to the rail and point and say to each other *will you look at that moon? Isn't it amazing?* Because this evening the moon doesn't look like a fingernail paring or a white goddess or cheese. It looks like something from outer space. See how its shading shows craters and contours. If you would only look up, you could see beyond the moon's beauty to the truth that you are a tiny creature living in a tiny garden that is hurtling through mostly empty space. You never got kicked out of Eden — you are living HERE!

But if you do get kicked out in the near future in some kind of tin can shot into space, it will be you who is doing the kicking after you've finished carbonating the ocean and the atmosphere. No angel with a blazing sword just you — burning and burning and burning.

Oh stop. STOP. Look up. Look at the moon.

Last Morning

Listen.
It is still not too late.

The invisible bird is a song
you can almost see, a shape
that hovers over the meadow,
absence above the swinging
blackberry cane.

Even now, as close as
the world,
it sings to you.

Acknowledgements

Many thanks for the generosity of all involved with the Ross and Davis Mitchell Prize for Faith and Poetry 2019 for choosing *Vigil*, my suite of fourteen poems which makes up the first section of this collection. Also to the Vancouver Writers Fest Poetry Contest, "Making Beds with Cordelia," the Short Grain Contest, "Matryoshka, Nesting Doll" and Whistler Village's Poet's Pause, "Sword Ferns in Spring"— abundant thanks for prizes and publication.

Thank you to literary journals *Arc, CV2, Grain, SubTerrain, The Antigonish Review, Pulp Literature, Understorey, Crux, Image, The High Window* (UK), *Broadview,* and *In/Words* for publishing many of these poems. I am thrilled that "Canticle for Sea Lions in Howe Sound" has made the leap from the page to a YouTube video by Bob Turner and is included in *Exploring Bowen's Marine World: a Marine Atlas of Nex̱wlélex̱wem/Bowen Island*.

To the League of Canadian Poets' *Poetry Pause* and to *Sweet Water: Poems for the Watershed* and its editor Yvonne Blomer — thank you for including my work and all you do for poetry.

An enormous thank you to my mentors and teachers who inspire me and offered tools to shape awkward early drafts into poems — the late Patrick Lane, Laura Apol, Jan Zwicky, and especially the magnificent Lorna Crozier.

Thanks to my daughter, Libby Osler, and my fellow poets, too many to name, for creating spaces for poetry and for your listening and responses.

Thank you to Jackie and Al Forrie at Thistledown Press for this second book, and to my editor, Seán Virgo, for your warmth, sharp eye and sparkling wit.

And to Emmett Sparling, adventurer/photographer/Instagram sensation for my cover photo.

To Ross, my love, deepest thanks for your unwavering enthusiasm, encouragement, for all of it.

The epigraph at the beginning of the book comes from the poem "Star Cluster" by Lorna Crozier in *The House the Spirit Builds*, Douglas & McIntyre: 2019.

One last word of gratitude goes out to the glorious fjord where I live and work, its many species and spectacles, its cloud and rain, sun and wind. Howe Sound/Atl'ka7tsem is the traditional and unceded territory of the Squamish people.